Coloring Book

ANIMALS
of
EUROPE

Mark Shawe

Book Series: Animal Planet

In this Coloring Book you will find:

- 20 original realistic full-page images of wild animals of Europe on single-sided sheets to prevent bleed-through
- 60 interesting unusual facts about the animals

Grab you favorite tool: pencils, crayons, markers or paints, and start coloring!

ISBN: 9781079222258

WORLD MAP

Foxes

Foxes are primarily nocturnal animals that means they like to hunt at night. This means that they sleep during the day. It can change, though, depending on where the fox live.

Foxes are great night-time predators because their eyes are specially adapted to night vision.

Foxes are also very fast. They can run up to 65 kph (40 mph).

Foxes are omnivore animals and this means that they eat meat as well as vegetation.

life expectancy in nature

weigh up to   10 kg (22 lb)

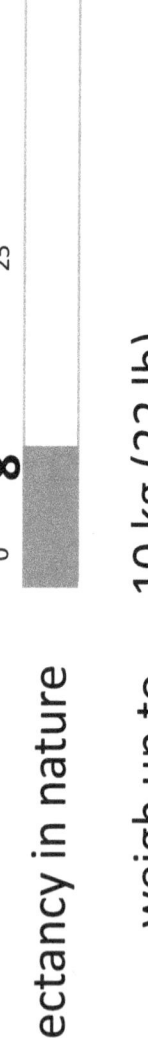

0   8   25   50   75   100

Red deer

Red deer are ruminant animals and therefore regurgitate their food and remasticate to aid in digestion. (Wow, lots of big words here!) This habit is also known as chewing cud.

Red deer browse in the early morning and late evening. They are inactive during the day and the middle of the night, when they spend most of their time chewing their cud.

Red deer are social animals; they live in summer herds with as many as 400 individuals. These herds are matriarchal and are dominated by a single cow.

life expectancy in nature

| 0 | **20** | 25 | 50 | 75 | 100 |

weigh up to   170 kg (365 lb)

Alpine mountain goat

Mountain goats are the largest mammals found in their high-altitude habitats, which can exceed elevations of 4,000 meters (13,000 feet).

With a body built for climbing, the mountain goat is a particularly speedy animal when navigating rocky, uneven vertical terrain. A mountain goat can climb more than 450 meters vertical meters (1,500 feet) in 20 minutes — that's higher than the Empire State Building, and he does it without stairs! (Not to be tried by kids under 18!:)

life expectancy in nature

0   **10**   25   50   75   100

weigh up to   120 kg (245 lb)

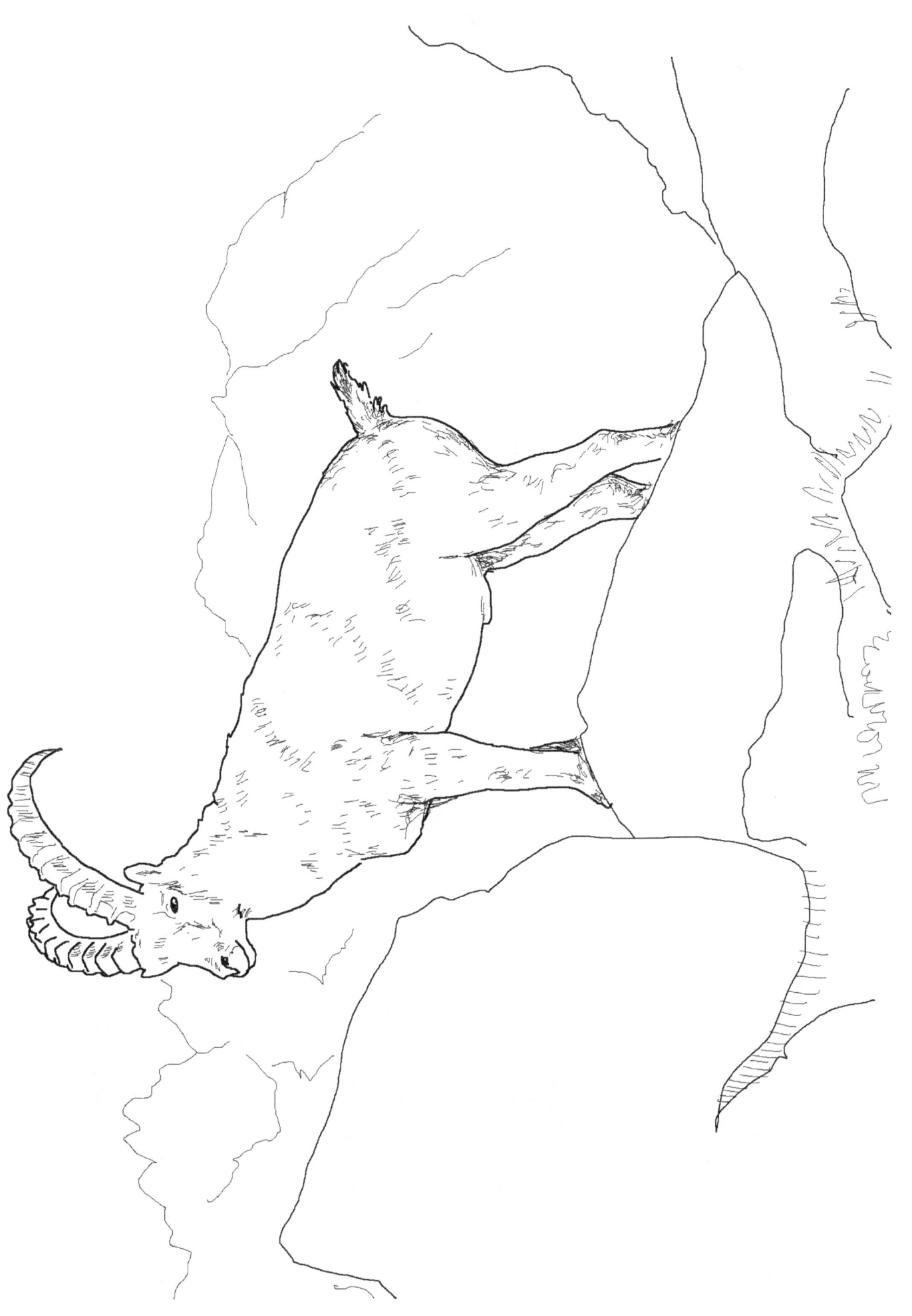

Brown bear

The brown bear is a naturally long-lived animal. The average lifespan in the wild is about 30 years. The oldest wild brown bear on record was nearly 37 years old. The oldest brown bear in captivity has been verified to live up to 47 years, with one captive male possibly being 50 years of age.

Despite their enormous size, brown bears are extremely fast, having been registered at speeds of 50 km (30 miles) per hour.

life expectancy in nature

weigh up to   450 kg (990 lb)

Wild rabbit

Rabbits have an excellent sense of smell, hearing and vision. They have nearly 360° panoramic vision, allowing them to detect predators from all directions. They can see everything behind them and only have a small blind-spot in front of their nose.

Rabbits have extremely strong hind limbs which allow them to leap great distances. They can jump up to one meter (3.3 feet) high and three meters (9.8 feet) long.

They are natural runners and can reach speeds of up to 60 kilometers per hour (37 miles per hour).

life expectancy in nature

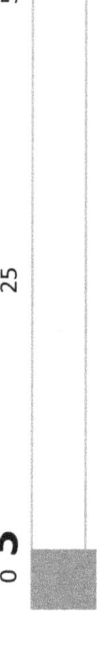

0   3   25   50   75   100

weigh up to   2,5 kg (5 lb)

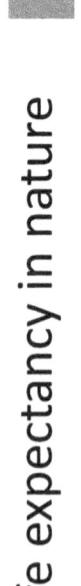

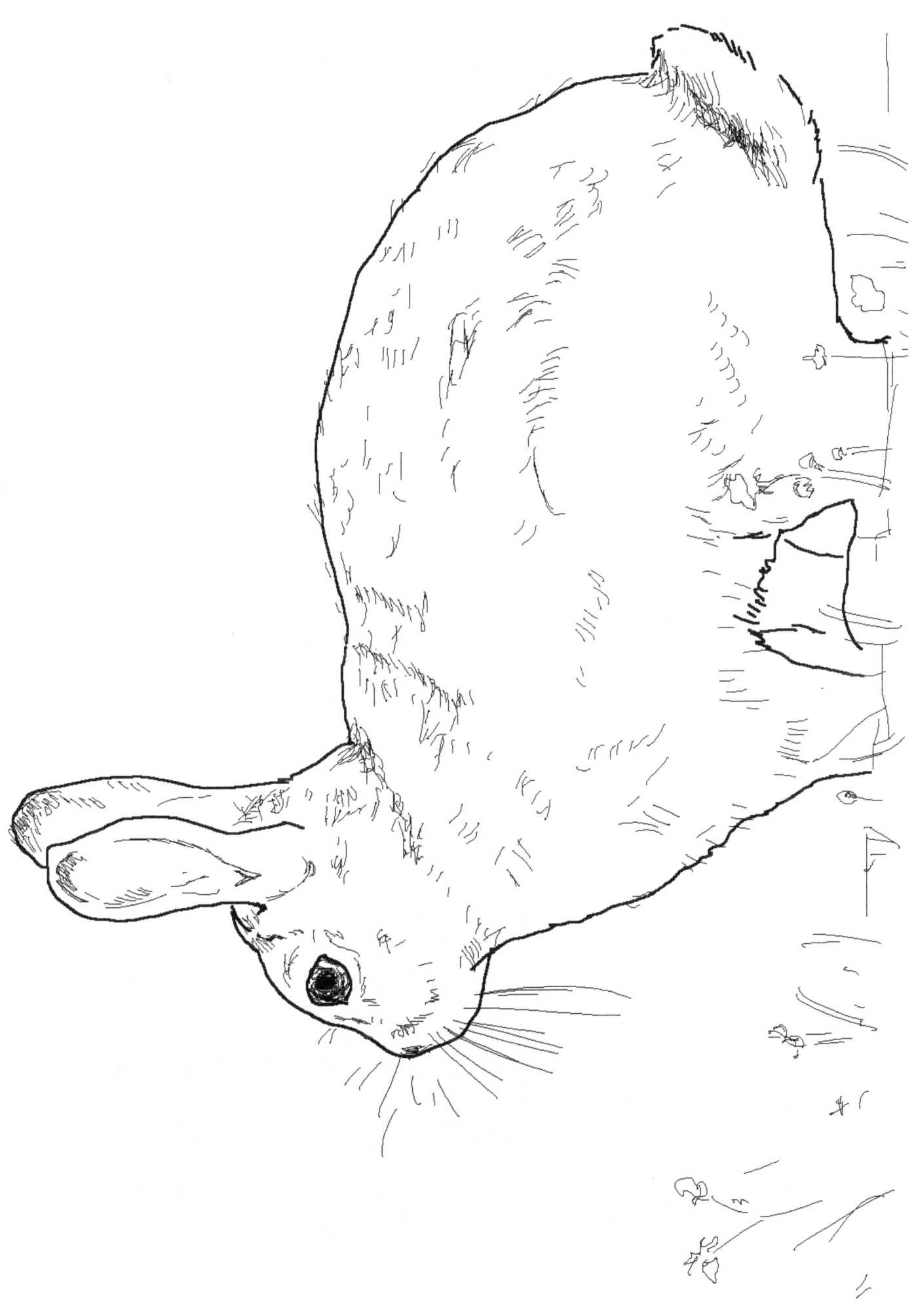

Wild boar, hog

Its sense of smell is very well developed to the point that the animal is used for drug detection in Germany. Its hearing is also acute, though its eyesight is comparatively weak, lacking colour vision and being unable to recognise a standing human 10–15 metres away. So, does that mean we are safe at that distance, or we'd better draw closer lest the hog takes us for his dinner opportunity?? Good question...

life expectancy in nature

| 0 | **12** | 25 | 50 | 75 | 100 |

weigh up to   120 kg (245 lb)

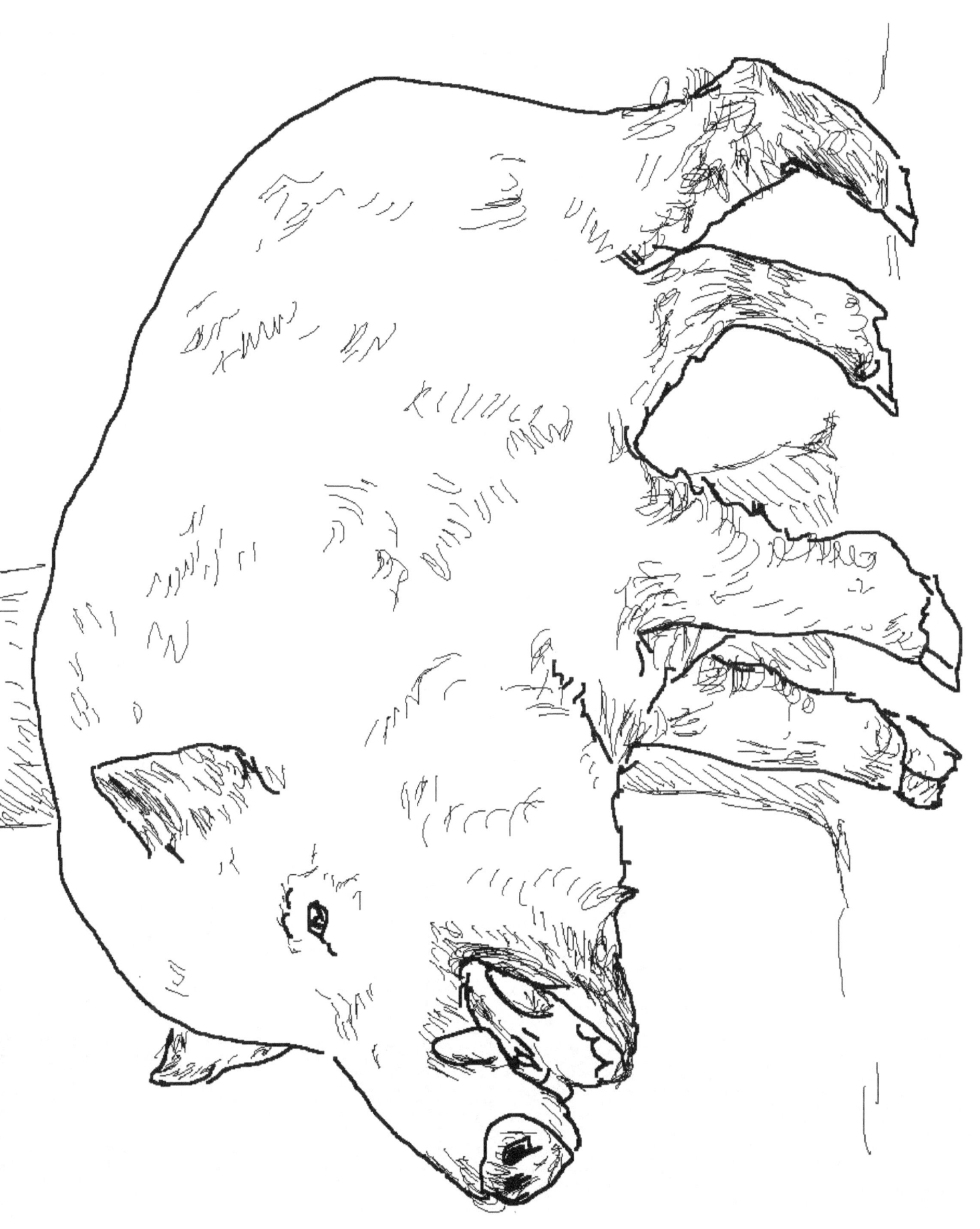

Ferret

Like dogs, ferrets have long canine teeth. Like cats, ferrets can be litterbox trained. (Now, that's convenient!) Ferrets, like cats, are pure carnivores that need a high quantity of protein and fat in their diet.

Ferrets usually interact with cats and dogs in a friendly manner. (Yessss!)

life expectancy in nature

0 **8** 25 50 75 100

weigh up to   0,8 kg (1,5 lb)

Hedgehog

Going into big numbers! Hedgehogs have about 5,000 – 7,000 spikes! Each spike lasts about a year then drops out and a replacement grows.

Some hedgehogs dig burrows in the soil up to 50 centimeters (20 inches) deep. Others prefer to make nests with dead leaves, grasses, and branches. Desert hedgehogs hide between boulders or burrow into the sand to escape the desert heat. In Asia, long-eared hedgehogs often move into burrows left by turtles, foxes, gerbils, and otters.

life expectancy in nature

| 0 | 5 | 25 | 50 | 75 | 100 |

weigh up to   1 kg (2 lb)

Musk ox

In the summer, musk oxen often feed near water, eating throughout the daylight hours to store up fat for the winter.

Musk-oxen are social animals and are usually found in herds. Herds can be as small as 3 animals or as large as 100 animals. Usually there are about 15 animals in a herd.

life expectancy in nature

| 0 | **16** | 25 | 50 | 75 | 100 |

weigh up to   600 kg (1320 lb)

Gray wolf

The gray wolf's head is large and heavy, with a wide forehead, strong jaws and a long, blunt muzzle. They have 42 teeth altogether. The gray wolf can reach a top speed of about 60 kilometers (37 miles) per hour in short bursts. It can leap 5 meters (16 feet) horizontally in a single jump. Wolves have a sense of hearing twenty times sharper than a human's and have a sense of smell a hundred times keener.

life expectancy in nature

0   8   25   50   75   100

weigh up to   55 kg (130 lb)

Reindeer

A male's antlers can measure up to 130 centimeters (51 inches) long, and a female's antlers can reach 50 centimeters (20 inches).

They are the only type of deer in which both male and female reindeer have antlers.

Reindeer have a strong sense of smell, and it's that sense of smell that assist them in finding the lichen under the snow. They can sniff out the plant material easily, even through snow that is 60 centimeters (23 inches) deep.

life expectancy in nature

weigh up to   200 kg (445 lb)

0   **20**   25   50   75   100

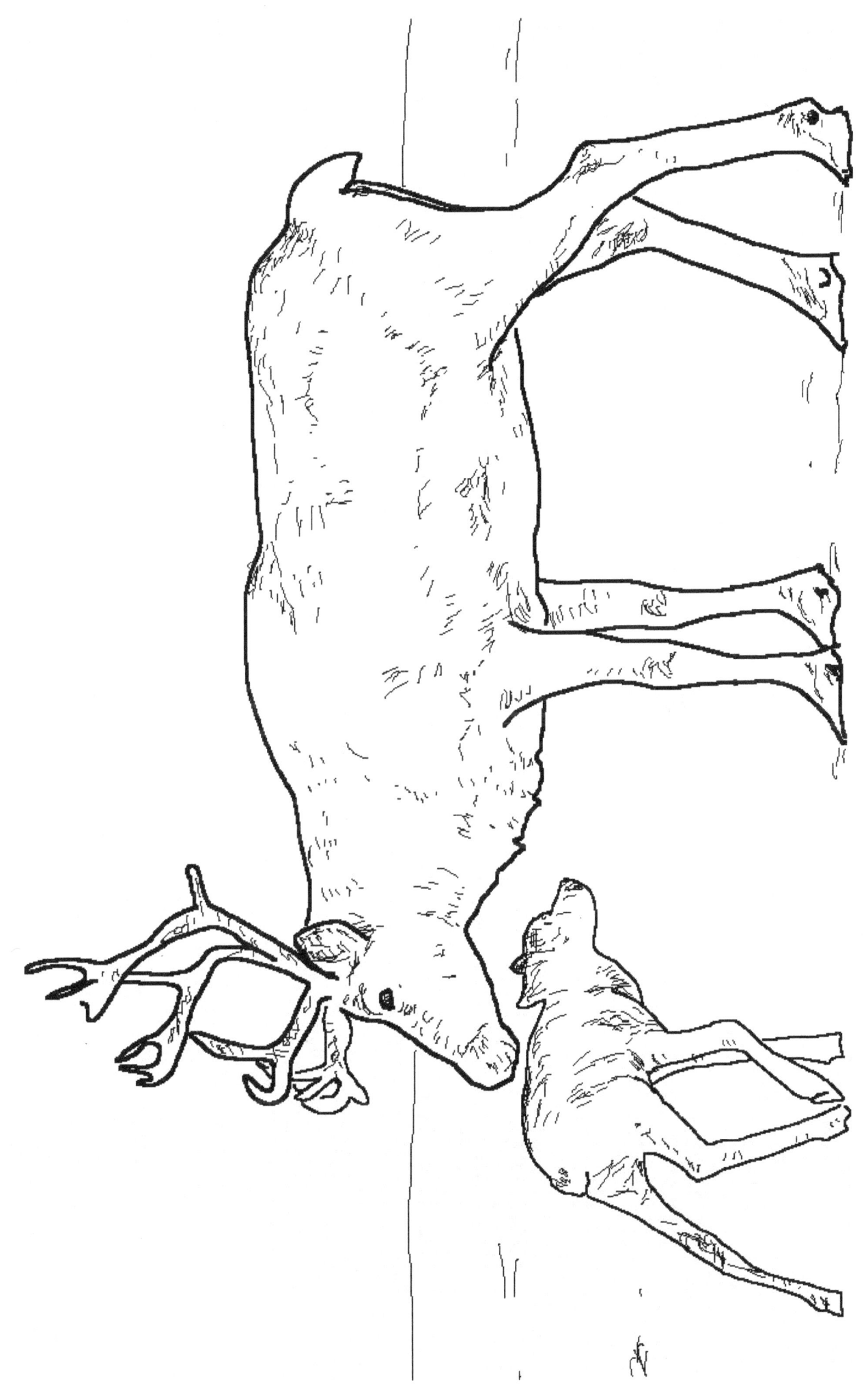

Badger

Badgers have acute hearing and excellent sense of smell, which helps them find food, but their eyes are small and their eyesight is not very good.

But their cutest feature is that they are incredibly clean and will not defecate in their sett – they have special latrines (communal toilets) comprising of shallow pits placed away from the setts on the edge of their territory. They will not bring food into the sett either. (Do you bring food into your bedroom???)

life expectancy in nature

0   **12**   25   50   75   100

weigh up to   24 kg (50 lb)

Owl

The average lifespan of the barred owl is about 10 to 12 years in the wild. The longest recorded age of a wild barred owl is 24 years.

Their diet consists mainly of small mammals, but they are also known to prey upon other small animals such as birds, reptiles, amphibians and other small animals.

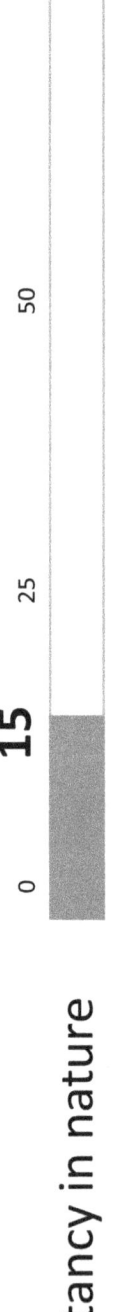

0   **15**   25   50   75   100

life expectancy in nature

weigh up to   2,5 kg (5 lb)

Jerboa

Jerboas look somewhat like miniature kangaroos, and have some external similarities. Both have long hind legs, very short forelegs, and long tails. Jerboas move around in a similar manner to kangaroos, which is by hopping.

Related jerboas often create four types of burrows. A temporary, summer day burrow is used for cover while hunting during the daylight. They have a second, temporary burrow used for hunting at night. They also have two permanent burrows: one for summer and one for winter. The permanent summer burrow is actively used throughout the summer and the young are raised there. Jerboas hibernate during the winter and use the permanent winter burrow for this. Temporary burrows are shorter in length than permanent burrows

life expectancy in nature

0   3   25   50   75   100

weigh up to   0,1 kg (0,25 lb)

Arctic fox

An Arctic fox can survive in extremely low temperatures, sometimes reach as low as -50 °C (-58 °F)! Brrrr!

The Arctic fox can run at the speed of around 48 kilometers (30 miles) per hour.

The Arctic fox is the only land mammal native to Iceland. It came to the isolated North Atlantic island at the end of the last ice age, walking over the frozen sea.

life expectancy in nature

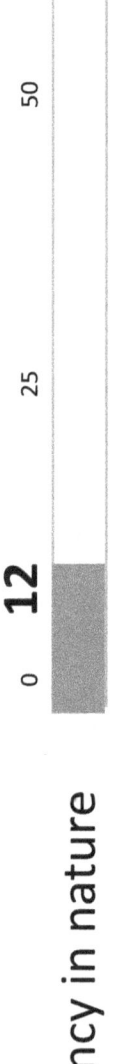

12

0   25   50   75   100

weigh up to   6 kg (13 lb)

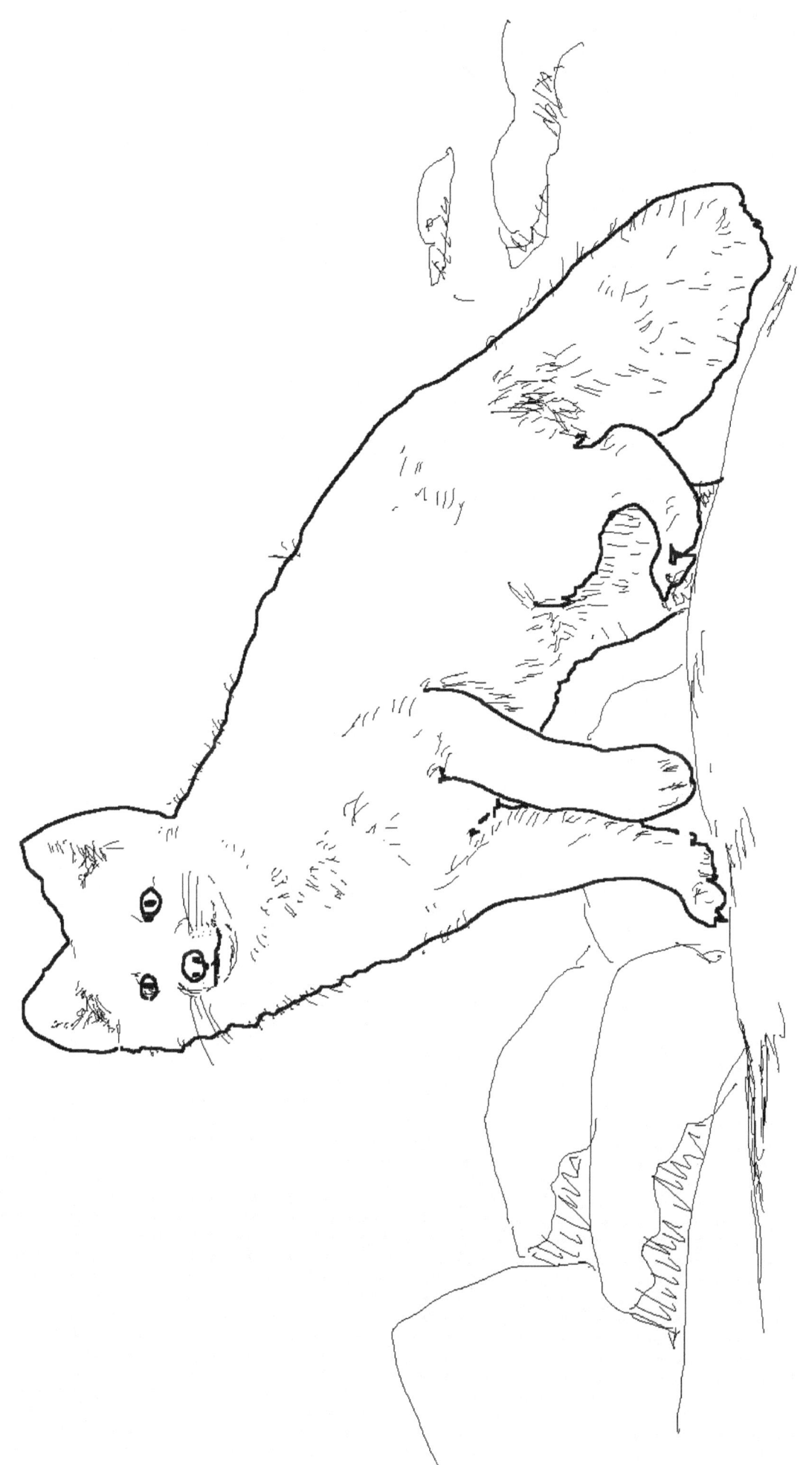

Long-faced seal

They have well-developed senses — their eyesight and hearing are adapted for both air and water.

Seals dive for three minutes at a time typically, and most species can stay under water for up to 30 minutes. But champion divers, such as elephant seals hold their breath for about 2 hours! That's what they should call true free diving!

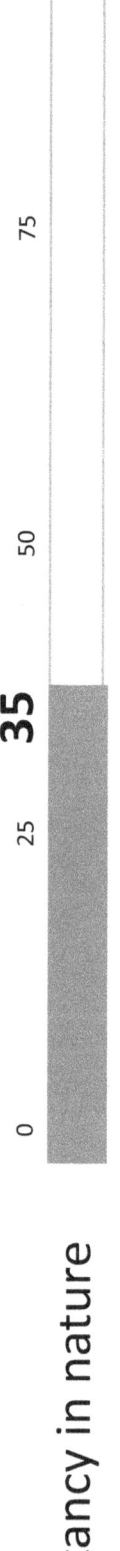

life expectancy in nature

35

0   25   50   75   100

weigh up to   310 kg (685 lb)

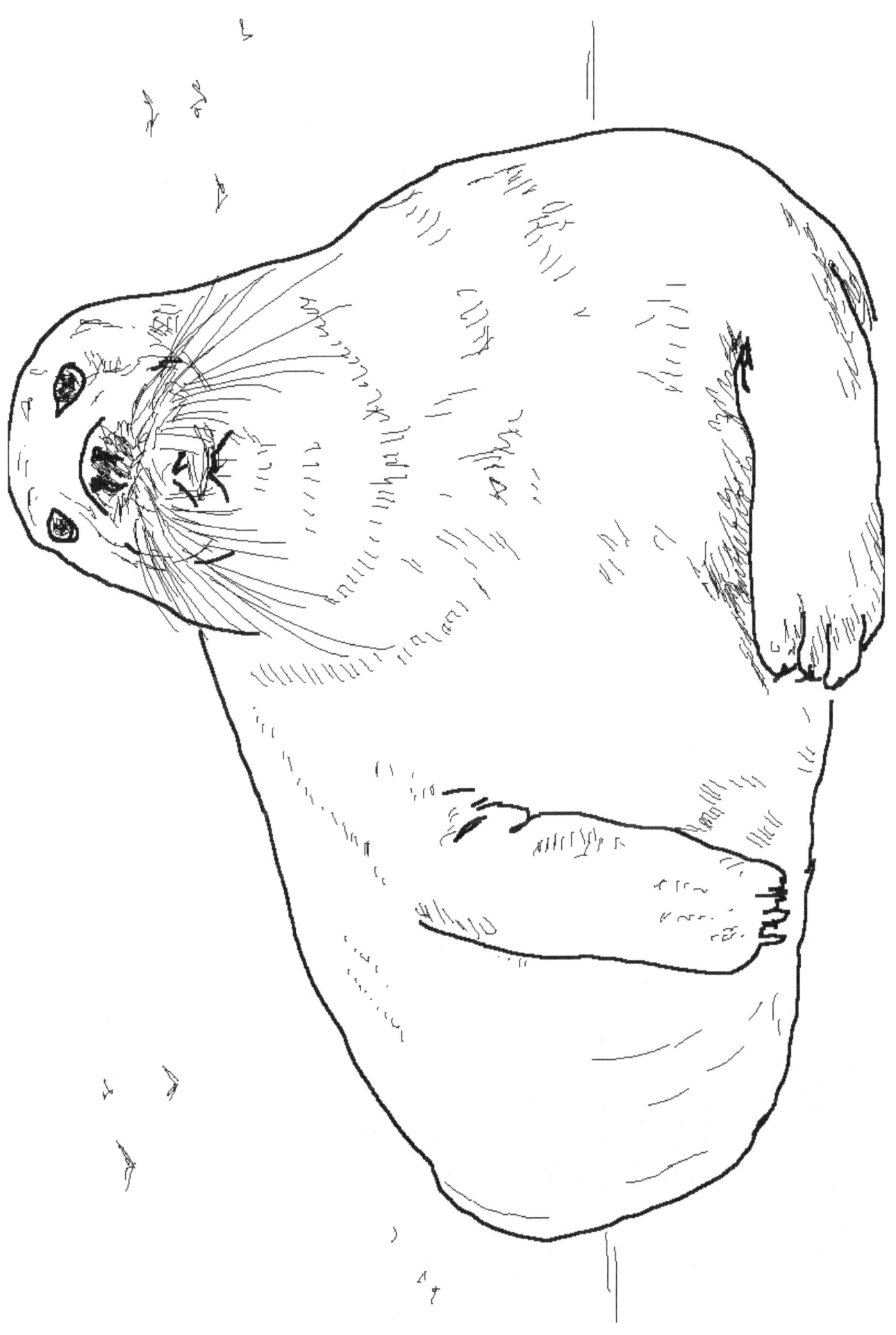

Great spotted woodpecker

The tongue of a woodpecker is up to 10 centimeters (4 inches) long and three times the length of its bill. Many woodpeckers have barbed tongues that help them extract bugs from trees and holes. When the long tongue is not in use, the woodpecker wraps it around the back of its head, between the skull and the skin.

Strong, dense muscles in the bird's neck give it strength to repeatedly thump its head. But it is extra muscles in the skull that keep the bird from getting hurt. These muscles act like a protective helmet for the brain.

Unlike the human brain , the woodpecker's brain is tightly confined by muscles in the skull and a compressible bone. This keeps the woodpecker brain from jiggling around when the bird is stabbing away at a tree trunk.

Woodpecker is able to peck 20 times per second. It produces between 10,000 and 12,000 pecks per day.

life expectancy in nature

0	**10**	25	50	75	100

weigh up to   0.1 kg (0.2 lb)

Fire salamander

Salamanders are capable of regenerating lost limbs, as well as other damaged parts of their bodies. They routinely regenerate complex tissues. (Omg, imagine all the fun stuff you could do having this kind of ability?)

Salamanders can drop their tail to escape predators. The tail will drop off and wriggle around for a little while, and the salamanders will either run away or stay still enough to not be noticed while the predator is distracted.

The skin of some species contains the powerful poison tetrodotoxin; these salamanders tend to have bright warning coloration.

life expectancy in nature

14

0   25   50   75   100

weigh up to   0,04 kg (0,08 lb)

Perch

The European perch is found in Europe and Asia. This species is typically greenish in color with dark vertical bars on its sides with a red or orange coloring in the tips of its fins.

Perch are popular sport fish species. They are known to put up a fight, and to be good eating. Yam-yam!

life expectancy in nature

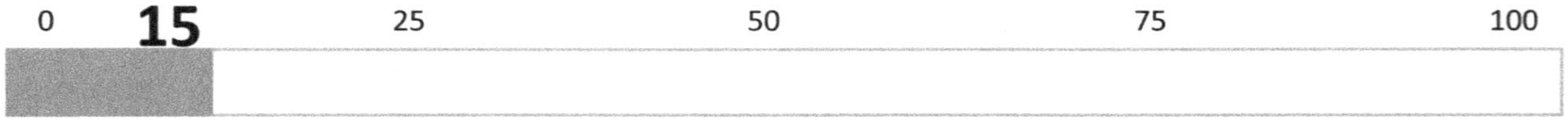

0   **15**   25   50   75   100

weigh up to   1 kg (2 lb)

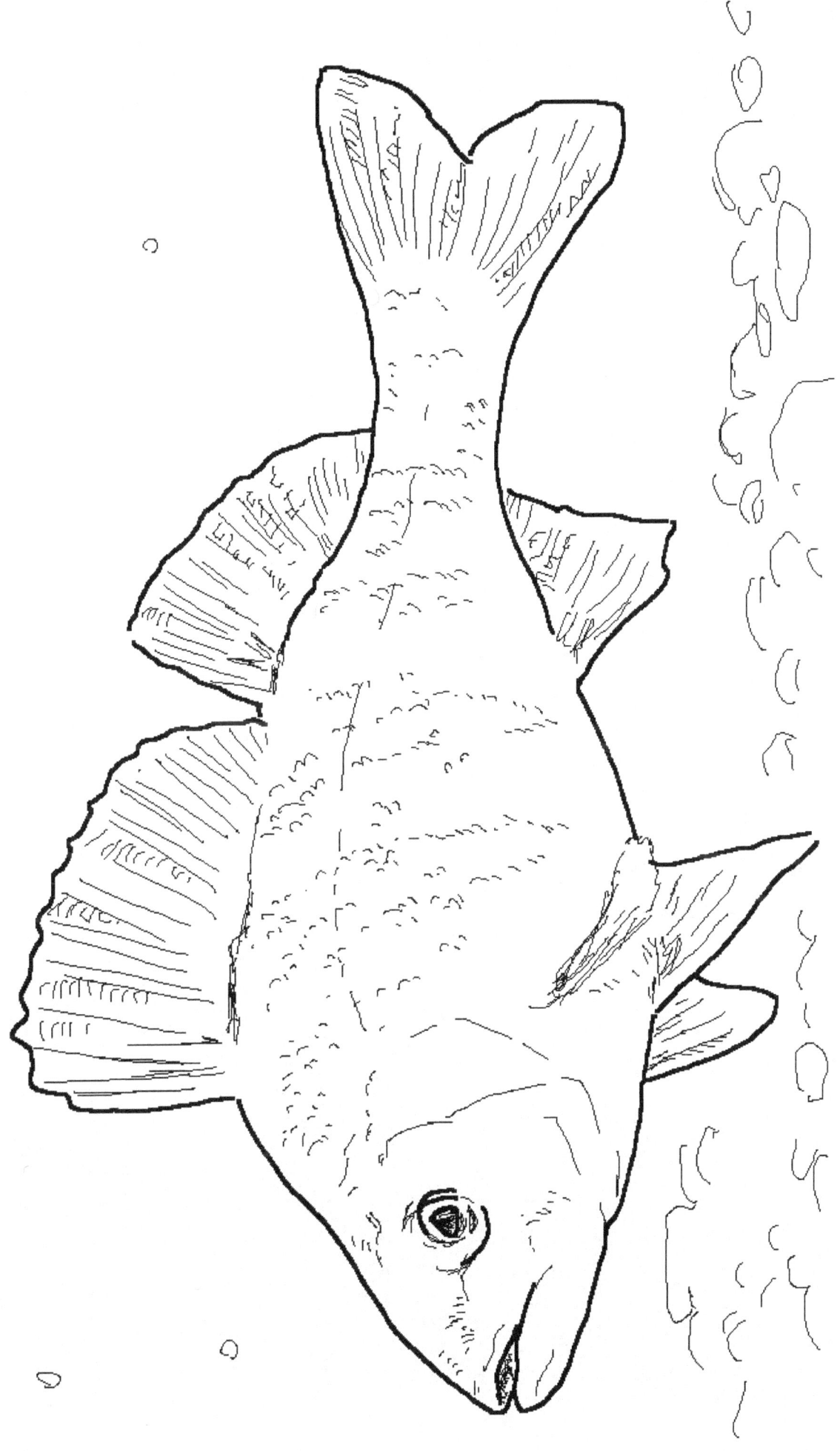

Squirrel

Squirrels are extremely intelligent creatures. They are known to put on elaborate bogus food burying displays to deceive onlookers. The fake burials are to trick potential thieves, such as other squirrels or birds, into thinking that they have stored their food stock there. Any observers planning on taking the stash will then focus on the bogus burial site, allowing the squirrel to bury the real stash elsewhere safely.

Squirrels don't dig up all of their buried nuts, which results in more trees!

The squirrel is the Native American symbol for preparation, trust and thriftiness. They easily make friends with people who feed them in the parks and are always ready for some running-around-the-tree game!

life expectancy in nature

weigh up to   0,3 kg (0,6 lb)

Dear Reader!

Thank you for choosing my book! Hope you enjoyed it!

If you really liked it, please, **leave a short review on Amazon!**
Use ISBN # 9781079222258 to find this book

Check out my website http://21centurywritersclub.com/ for more
books by me and my fellow writers!

See ya,
Mark

SEARCH MORE COLORING BOOKS

Book Series: **Animal Planet**

Animals of Australia

ISBN # 9781079226393

Animals of South America

ISBN # 9781079222920

Animals of Asia

ISBN # 9781079224740

Animals of North America

ISBN # 9781079225525

Animals of Antarctica

ISBN # 9781079225969

Animals of Africa

ISBN # 9781079227536

SPECIAL EDITION

COLORING BOOK:
ANIMALS OF THE WORLD

140 original realistic full-page images of wild animals of the World on single-sided sheets to prevent bleed-through

420 interesting unusual facts about the animals

ISBN # 9781079226799

Book Series: Animal Planet